LOGOS, DOULOS & LOGOS II

THE STORY OF THREE REMARKABLE SHIPS

ISBN 1 85985 035 9
Copyright © 1994 OM Ships

First published in 1994 by Candle Books Ltd

Distributed by STL
PO Box 300, Carlisle, CA3 0JH

All rights reserved. No part of this publication may be reproduced or transmitted in any form or by any means, electronic or mechanical, including photocopying, recording, or any information storage or retrieval system, without either prior permission in writing from the publisher or a licence permitting restricted copying.

Designed and created by
Three's Company,
12 Flitcroft Street,
London WC2H 8DJ

Illustrations on front cover, pp. 12-13 (bottom) and 16-17 by Jeremy Gower; pp. 12-13 (top) by Tony Kenyon

Worldwide co-edition conceived organised and produced by
Angus Hudson Ltd,
Concorde House,
Grenville Place,
London NW7 3SA
Telephone: +44 81 959 3668
Fax: +44 81 959 3678

Printed in England

Welcome aboard!

Dear reader,

Welcome to the ship ministry!
Over the last few years I have heard several times something to this effect: 'The ships don't belong just to OM. They belong to us!' Absolutely right!
Those who make this statement are Christians who have prayed for and supported the ships. Many of them have never seen Logos, Logos II or Doulos, but still they feel identified with the ministry. They get excited about the fact that Logos II and Doulos together on a typical day have 4,000 visitors. Several hundred attend conferences on board or on shore. Many other people who never actually visit the ships learn about them through local TV, radio and newspaper coverage.
The ship co-workers come from about forty different nations. Our backgrounds, temperaments, abilities, personalities and education differ greatly. What draws us together is the message we share wherever we can: God loves people and invites us to a relationship with Him.
We hope you enjoy this presentation. Try to visit one of the ships sometime. It would be a pleasure to welcome you on board.
Wishing you enjoyable reading,

Dale Rhoton
Director, OM Ships

How it all began

'Holidays coming soon. Why don't we go to Mexico?'

'Great idea!' responded the little group of American college students enthusiastically.

Their dreams, however, were not of sun-drenched beaches or exotic foods. Their interest was people. God and people. They had made an exciting discovery: how to know God in a deeply personal way. This was too good to keep to themselves. They wanted to tell everyone. Mexico was close. Why not start there?

They did. Every vacation time. Other students joined them. Soon they branched out to Europe as well. No longer limiting their time to holidays, many began devoting a year or two to travelling and sharing their faith.

Everywhere the pattern was similar. They would sell or give away literature and simply talk with people: the mother in a park with her children, the friendly shop owner, the couple waiting for a bus, anyone who had time for a chat.

A ship?

When their leader, George Verwer (then in his mid-twenties), came up with the idea of a ship, his friends thought it was crazy.

'A ship? What would you do with a ship? You don't know the first thing about ships or sailing.'

George's response was to point to a map, saying, 'Look at how much of the world's population lives in port cities. We could transport our people and books to them with a ship and while we're at sea, our people could be studying together.'

Eventually he convinced enough people, and the search was on for a suitable ship. Not just any ship. Their ship had to be ocean-going and able to store enough food and water for long voyages. It had to contain space for a lecture hall, a book exhibition and storage of vehicles for inland travel. It had to accommodate at least 120 people. Above all, the price had to be right because the young people possessed very little money.

Almost ideal

Numerous ships were visited and dismissed as unsuitable. One of them was the Danish ship, *Umanak*. In spite of the rejection, its name popped up again and again. The ship seemed ideal in every way except one. It was designed for a cold climate and lacked the air-conditioning so important for life in hotter climates where much of the world's population live. After much thought, some engineers worked out a way to adapt the ventilation system for cooling. In September, 1970, negotiations were started to purchase the *Umanak*. The cost was £70,500 pounds.

George Verwer.

4

The Umanak.

The Logos story

In order to buy the ship, the young people needed to find £70,500 within one month – or lose their down-payment of £7000.

The Logos moored off Calcutta, India.

They had only £45,000 on hand from contributions for the project. A scary situation for a group of young people without financial resources. They could only pray hard that God would help them.

He did. Within one month they received donations for just the amount needed. On October 15, 1970, the ship became officially theirs. She was rechristened *Logos* ('Word' in Greek) and was towed off to Holland for a necessary overhaul and alterations.

Professional seamen and volunteers with a variety of skills came from many parts of the world to roll up their sleeves and plunge into the dirty, greasy job of preparing the ship for action. They did it all out of love for God; they received no pay whatever.

Other people donated special equipment or supplies needed for the ship and its crew.

First voyage

Finally, in February, 1971, *Logos* made the first voyage under her own steam as she sailed from Rotterdam to London. Visitors and friends who had heard about the ship streamed on board to see it. The ship's company was kept busy giving tours or loading supplies for the long voyage ahead of them.

A week later *Logos* set sail for India, calling in at Lagos, Nigeria and Cape Town, South Africa, en route. In each port a small book exhibition was set up on deck under an awning and the

The *Logos* at anchor.

public was invited aboard to buy books and attend meetings.

India at last!
The ship's company – largely young adults with a sprinkling of older, experienced officers – had hoped that many people would be interested enough to visit the ship, but they had a few secret doubts. To their amazement, crowds began flocking to the ship. As a matter of fact, in India so many people came that the ship's crew had to come up with ways to control the crowd. Local people were curious about the ship and hungry for the literature which could be purchased in the book exhibition.

After India came Indonesia. In the next seventeen years *Logos* visited a over one hundred countries. In 1972 she visited Bangladesh just after that country was created. In 1974 she sailed into war-torn Vietnam shortly before the collapse of Saigon. In 1981 she was able to enter China, although under considerable restriction. In 1982, in the midst of the Lebanon/Israel conflict, a cease-fire stopped the fighting for a couple of weeks, just long enough for a *Logos* visit. Everywhere the story was the same. People were eager to obtain literature and to talk with the international crew and staff of this unusual ship.

The captain of the Logos plots his course.

The Logos in dry dock.

The gangway to the Logos. EBE stands for Educational Book Exhibits.

Volunteers all

On the ships you will meet volunteers who come from all over the world. At any one time up to 500 volunteers from about forty different countries are working on the ships.

Some of the volunteers stand beside the ship's hull in dry dock.

Anyone who comes to work on one of the ships expecting an easy, blissful life is in for a shock.

Usually about 300 men and women serve on *Doulos* and just under 200 on *Logos II*. They come from 40-50 different countries. Two of the most recent nationalities to be added were Mongolian and Albanian. As you can well imagine, communication and mutual understanding sometimes become a problem, even though everyone who comes to work is required to speak English.

Some of the workers are serving in their professions –

8

the captain, deck and engine officers, doctors, carpenters, welders, teachers, administrators, secretaries, cooks, etc. A large proportion of the workers, however, come aboard with no skills or training for their assigned jobs. Most are in their late teens or twenties. The main qualification for them is a willingness to learn and to work hard.

Hard times
Life on board is not always easy. On most ships, the crew spends from a few weeks to several months on board and then has an extended vacation ashore to recuperate; on *Doulos* and *Logos II*, everyone lives the year round on board. Work can be demanding, the hours long. The workers have to learn to adjust to different climates (often very hot ones), cultures, customs and foods. They have to learn to live harmoniously in a tiny, crowded cabin with people of different temperaments and habits. At sea, those who are untroubled by violent pitching and tossing of waves often have to step in and assume the work of their less fortunate comrades with green faces and queasy stomachs.

All this for what? Not for a big salary. Everyone on board is a volunteer. Apart from a little pocket money, no one – not even the captain – receives any pay. What motivates these people is a love for God and for their fellow men and women, and a desire to use their lives to help the peoples of the world.

Everyone on board works hard to keep the ship running and to care for the people aboard. There is still time and energy for extra things, however, such as participating in a Bible study programme or going ashore periodically to be involved in meetings in schools, prisons, churches, hospitals or even in the open air. The ship's company present programmes on board as well, often dressing in their national costumes and telling something about their countries' culture or entertaining with a folk-song or dance.

A crew member explains the Bible to a visitor.

Rewards
One of the most prized experiences of ship personnel is getting to know local people and forming friendships that last long after the ship has moved on. They enjoy the opportunity to tell about meaningful experiences they have had with God and to offer hope and encouragement to people whose lives are twisted, shattered, or simply empty and meaningless.

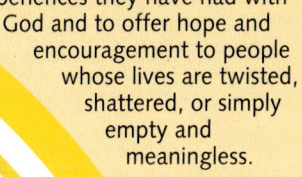

9

LOGOS

The *Umanak* (2,319 tons and 82 metres long) was built in Denmark in 1949 to sail in the waters around Greenland.

During the seventeen years as *Logos*, she sailed 231,250 nautical miles and visited ports in 103 different countries. In that time about 51,000,000 books and leaflets (including 450,000 Bibles and New Testaments) were sold or given away.

Shipwreck

Shortly before midnight on January 4, 1988, tragedy struck.

Logos had left the port of Ushuaia in the southernmost part of Argentina and was sailing through the Beagle Channel. The pilot, anxious to avoid the rough waters of a brewing storm outside, asked to be allowed to leave while the ship was still in sheltered waters. He hastily pointed out a safe route for the captain before disembarking on a small boat waiting for him. A few minutes later *Logos* was swept off course by a combination of currents and strong winds. At 11:56 p.m. she struck a submerged rock and remained aground, in spite of all the efforts of the captain and his officers to free her.

Distress calls

At this point the ship was in Chilean waters. The Chilean Navy stationed nearby had heard the distress calls and sent naval vessels out to offer assistance if needed. It was needed. At 5:10 a.m., when it became apparent that *Logos* could not be saved, her captain finally gave the order to abandon ship.

With much difficulty, because the ship was listing far to one side, the life boats were lowered. Crew and staff – including a mother with a six-week-old baby – calmly climbed into the boats just as they had been taught in the weekly boat drills.

There was no panic or injury as the boats were lowered into the freezing water. Twenty minutes later everyone was safely on board the Chilean naval vessels and on their way to the naval base at Puerto Williams where they were received with great kindness.

Saved

Gone was the ship that had served for seventeen years. Gone were the possessions, the photos, all the personal mementos of the ship's company. But safe was the most important part of all – the people.

Lifebelts for everyone!

The Logos grounded in the Beagle Channel.

'Abandon ship!'

Everyone was safe.

Running the ships

By the time a ship is a couple of decades old, she usually begins to show her age. Many large shipping companies find the upkeep becomes too expensive to be cost-effective and start looking for a new ship as a replacement.

Doulos was built in 1914 and *Logos II* in 1968. While meeting the rigorous international safety standards required by Malta, their country of registration, they nevertheless demand a great deal of maintenance work. Volunteer labour makes this possible, along with donations of money and materials. (Just to repaint *Doulos* each year requires about 3,700 litres of paint.)

Fuel is obviously an important, as well as an expensive, item in running a ship. *Doulos'* fuel costs were greatly reduced in 1984 by installing a new generator that operates on the same cheaper grade of fuel as the main engine. Fuel is not just the power-provider for voyages; it is necessary as well while the ship is in port because it provides for the electrical needs of the community living aboard: air heating, air-conditioning, water supply, lighting, cooking, etc. Without fuel, the ship becomes a silent, lifeless shell.

The same community that requires power from fuel also has to eat. On *Doulos* alone, that means about 1,000 meals a day must be served. To prepare meals, the cooks must have food. The chief steward buys many things ashore in each port, including fresh fruit and vegetables. Many other supplies are sent out from Europe, where they are cheaper or more easily obtainable. Foresight and careful planning are essential.

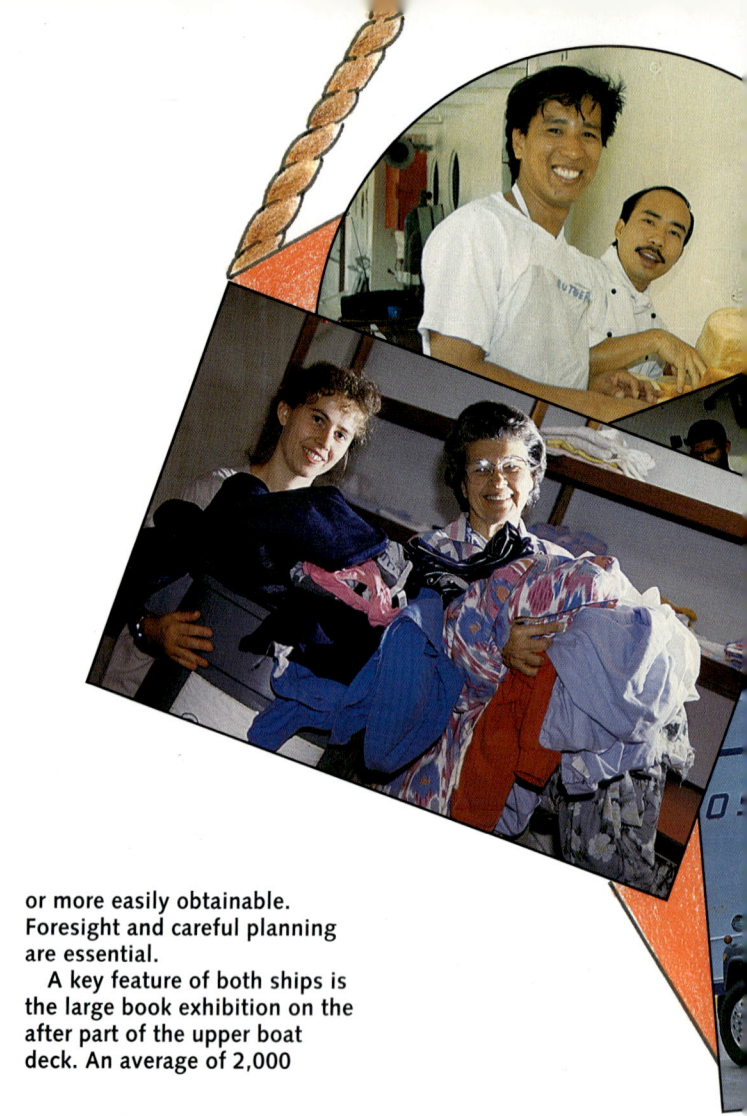

A key feature of both ships is the large book exhibition on the after part of the upper boat deck. An average of 2,000

1,000 meals served every day on Doulos.

50 loaves baked per day on Doulos.

3,700 litres of paint used every year.

200-250 pairs of shoes repaired every year.

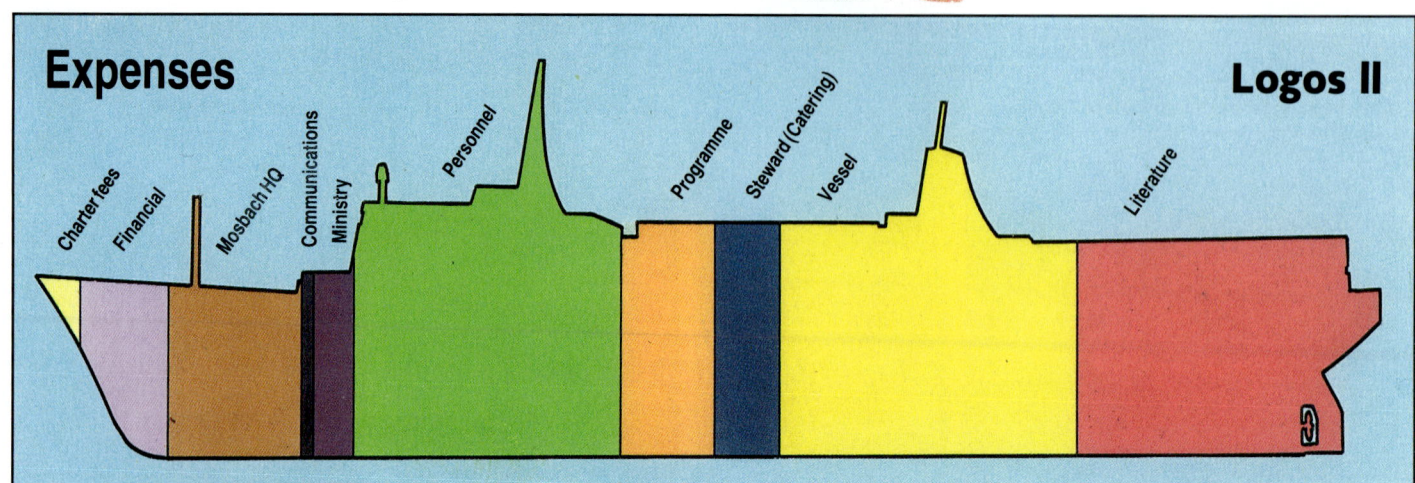

Expenses — Logos II

Charter fees · Financial · Mosbach HQ · Communications · Ministry · Personnel · Programme · Steward (Catering) · Vessel · Literature

12

The educational book exhibition on the *Doulos*.

visitors pass through the book exhibition on each ship every day, to browse and select from among the 4,000 titles offered. In order to keep the shelves supplied, the ships' holds are usually stocked with up to 500,000 books.

Because most books are shipped from overseas (allow at least six weeks for delivery!), the stock must be carefully monitored and orders placed well in advance. As the ships are continually moving, calculations must be made to determine which port a ship will be visiting at the time the book shipment is due to arrive. Great is the confusion, extra work and expense when a shipment fails to arrive in time and misses the ship.

Crew members' average stay two years.

35-45 nationalities on board.

2,750 tons of fuel for both ships every year.

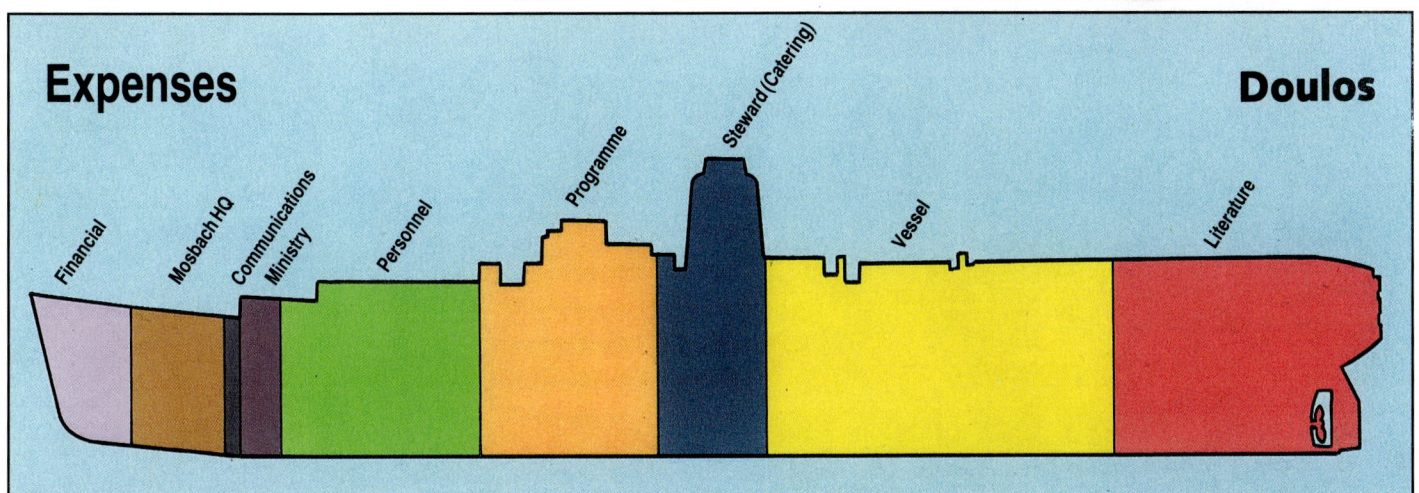

Expenses — Doulos

- Financial
- Mosbach HQ
- Communications Ministry
- Personnel
- Programme
- Steward (Catering)
- Vessel
- Literature

13

A community afloat

The crew of each ship have to plan for all the needs of everyday life while travelling miles out at sea.

The ships are not just work places; they are communities. In a way they are like small villages.

Each has its own 'restaurant', bakery, laundry, hospital, schools, playground, library, carpentry shop, barber's shop and general store, stocking small items such as toothpaste and snack food. There are also a print shop and – what ship people prize most – a post office where they can receive all those eagerly-awaited letters from home!

Visitors are sometimes surprised to see children playing on the ships, chatting happily with friends big and small. While most of the workers on the ships are young single men and women, there are a few families. Not

Members of the ship's catering team.

A crew member with a young visitor.

many, because cabin space is severely limited. A nursery caters for the younger children, while the older ones attend schools taught by qualified teachers and receive a most unusual education, reinforced by the wide variety of cultural experiences they get in travelling from country to country.

Village at sea
This village at sea has its unique aspects. Imagine working as a postal clerk in a post office that is located in a different country every few weeks, with constantly changing postal regulations and costs. Or the challenge of teaching a class consisting of only four or five youngsters, but each one of a different age, from a different country and at a different educational level! An institutional cook has a thankless task at best, but how about trying to meet the culinary expectations of thirty to forty different nationalities?

Adjusting
Needless to say, life on board is a constant exercise in adjusting and learning to appreciate people who differ in background, habits, tastes and expectations.

Office staff.

On-board school.

There is a nursery aboard ship.

M V Doulos

This specially commissioned cutaway illustration shows many of the unusual features on board the *Doulos*.
The ship has been very carefully converted to fulfil the unusual demands made upon it.

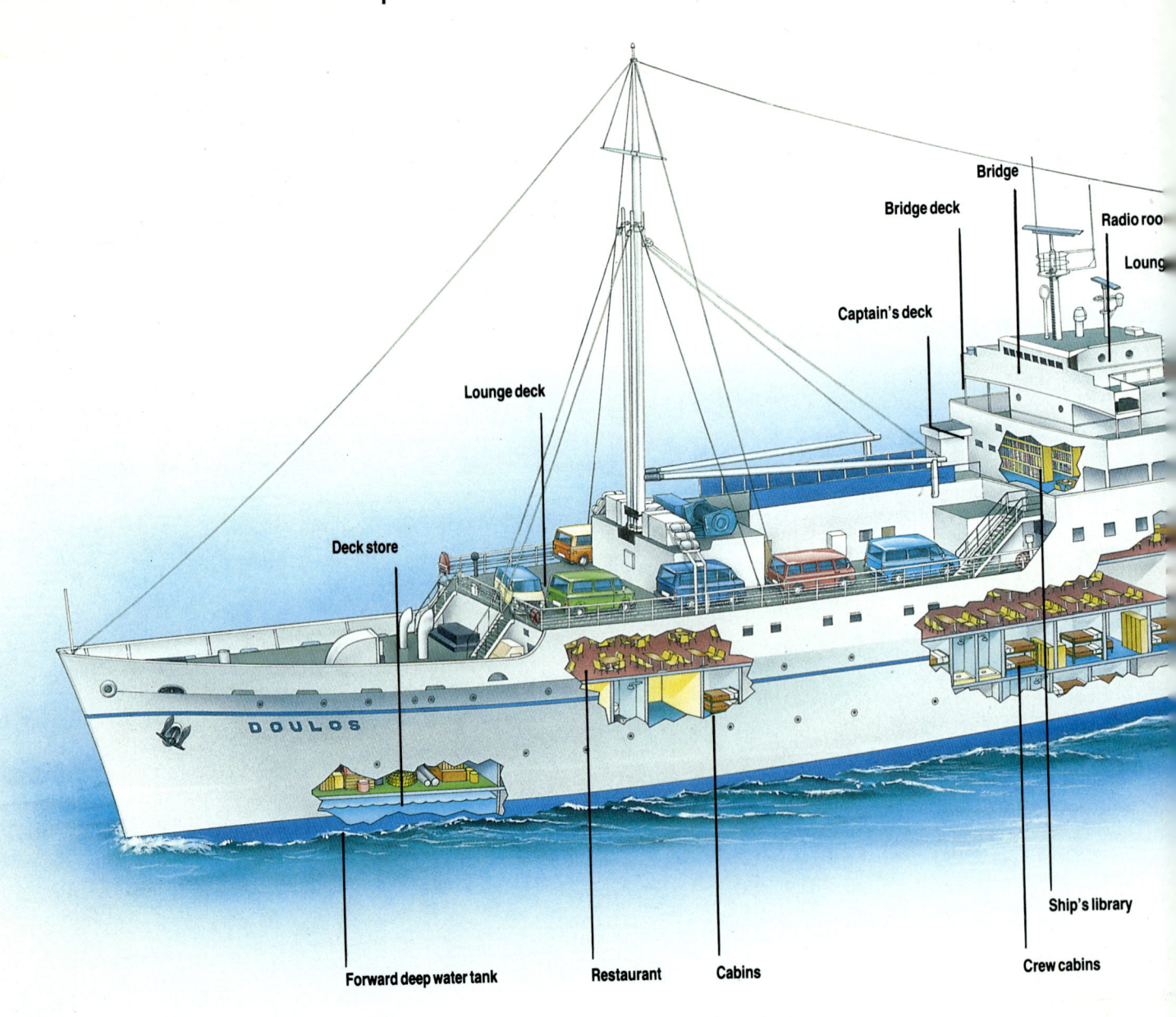

- Bridge
- Bridge deck
- Radio room
- Lounge
- Captain's deck
- Lounge deck
- Deck store
- Ship's library
- Crew cabins
- Forward deep water tank
- Restaurant
- Cabins

Moored in an idyllic setting.

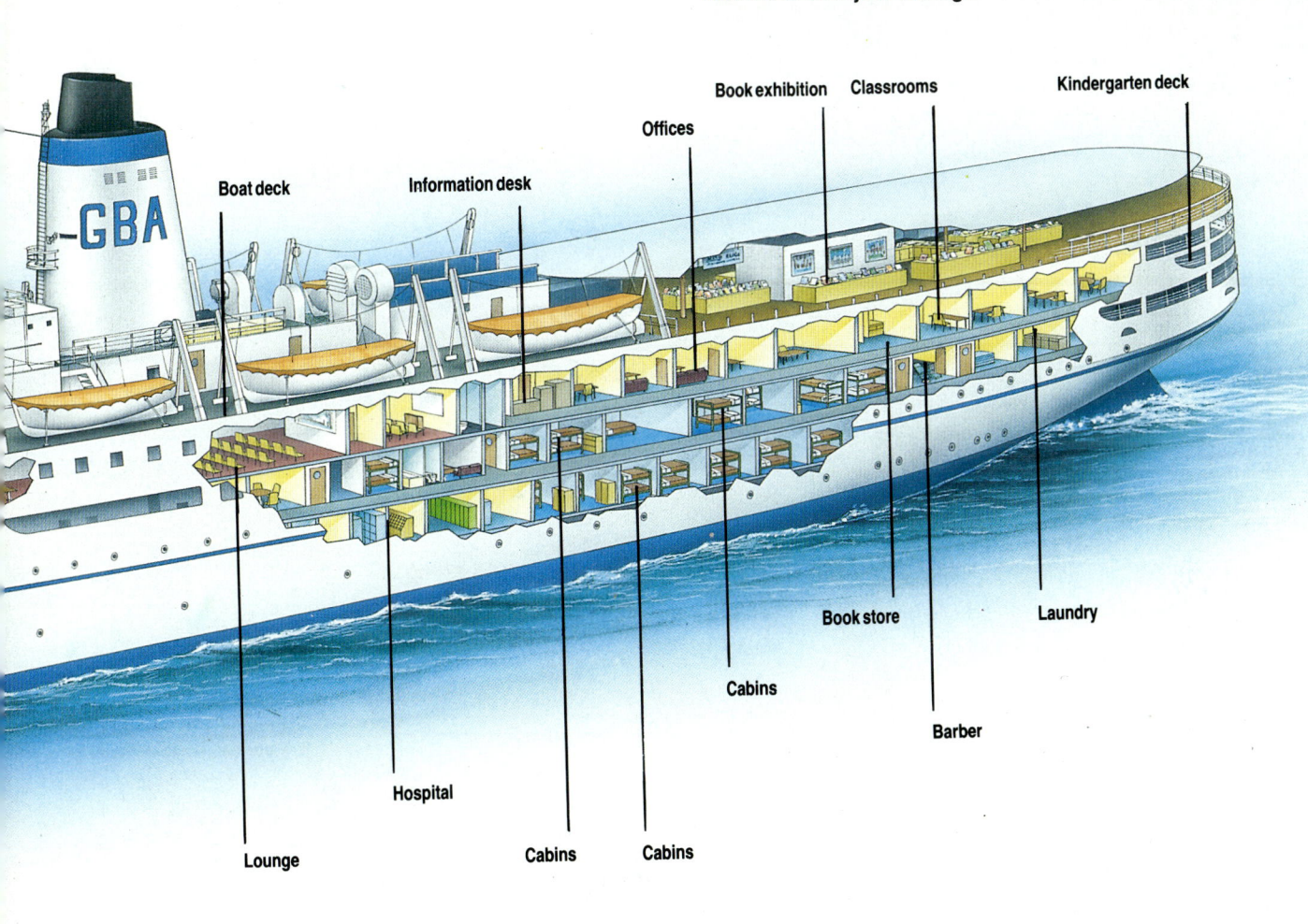

- Boat deck
- Information desk
- Offices
- Book exhibition
- Classrooms
- Kindergarten deck
- Book store
- Laundry
- Barber
- Cabins
- Hospital
- Cabins
- Cabins
- Lounge

17

The Doulos

By the time the *Logos* had been operating for six years, so many opportunities had opened up that the leaders began looking for another ship.

Logos was purchased in 1970. The venture proved such a success that her leaders began looking for another ship as well.

In 1977 they inspected Franca C, a 'grand old lady' built in 1914. Originally called *Medina,* the ship had been used for various things – including the transportation of vegetables – until she was finally converted into a luxury liner to cruise in the Mediterranean and Caribbean Seas.

Although an old ship (listed in 1992 in *The Guinness Book of Records* as the 'oldest active ocean-going passenger ship'), Franca C was solidly built and, with some major repairs, would be able to sail safely for many years. The size, layout and price were right. In December of 1977 she was purchased.

The *Medina* – now *Doulos*, the world's oldest ocean-going passenger ship.

Captain of the *Doulos*.

Queueing to board the *Doulos* in Bangkok, Thailand.

For the next six months she was laid up for repairs, alterations and restocking in Genoa and Bremen. In June, 1978, as *Logos* visited Asian ports, the 'new ship', renamed *Doulos* (Greek for 'servant'), set sail for France, Spain and eventually South America.

Larger than *Logos*, *Doulos* could accommodate more workers. With more space for her book exhibition, she could offer more titles. Whereas *Logos* could seat about 90 people for a conference, *Doulos* had places for more than 600.

The *Doulos* at Cape Town, South Africa.

Lending a helping hand

As the ships visit different countries, people on board are eager to help the many people they meet in any way they can.

A large book exhibition stocking more than 4,000 titles is one of the major attractions on each ship. Even in countries well supplied with bookshops, people come to browse and often discover literary 'treasures' they didn't know existed. However, in many of the countries visited by the ships, bookshops may be few in number and decidedly limited in stock. Book exhibition workers have been moved to see tears in the eyes of a teacher as she spotted a vitally needed textbook at nominal cost, or undisguised glee in the face of a child skipping off with a bright colouring book clutched to his or her breast.

Books for the people
For some countries where few people could afford the price of a new book, publishers have donated beautiful educational books to be distributed with only a small handling charge. Occasionally shipments of used books are also offered to the literature-starved public for a few cents. When *Logos* visited poverty-stricken Nicaragua in 1987, specially designated financial gifts made it possible for the ship to present pastors and other Christian leaders with key books to place on the shelves of their church libraries.

That's what the ships are all about. Helping people.

Physical help
Sometimes the help may be directed toward a physical need, as when *Doulos* brought relief goods to Mozambique and *Logos II* brought medical supplies to Nicaragua in 1992. Mostly, however, the help is in the form of providing information, training, encouragement and hope. Books are available on topics ranging from cookery to business management; film-shows, seminars and conferences offer help in the personal areas of life, covering a range of topics from marital counselling to building a relationship with God. Crew and staff alike enjoy forming friendships with individuals in the ports they visit and sharing life's experiences with its pains and joys.

Boat people

In October of 1980 in the South China Sea, *Logos* personnel spotted a tiny, rickety boat carrying refugees from Vietnam. Because of legal complications, the crew had been warned not to pick up refugees. *Logos* workers felt torn apart. They could not abandon these desperate people. In spite of possible problems, they welcomed the refugees on board, giving them food, clothing and medical care.

A second refugee boat appeared a few days later and was also accommodated by *Logos* crew. That meant 90 extra people on board a ship meant for 140!

The *Logos* crew had intended to tow the empty boats until land was sighted and then ask the refugees to make their own way ashore. That idea was scrapped, however, when it was discovered that both boats had sunk during a night at sea.

Complications
The warning about complications was justified, the *Logos* company discovered when they reached Thailand. For a month the Vietnamese refugees remained on board. Eventually Thai authorities were persuaded to accept them into the country.

Sampling the book exhibition.

The book exhibition boasts a wide range of helpful literature.

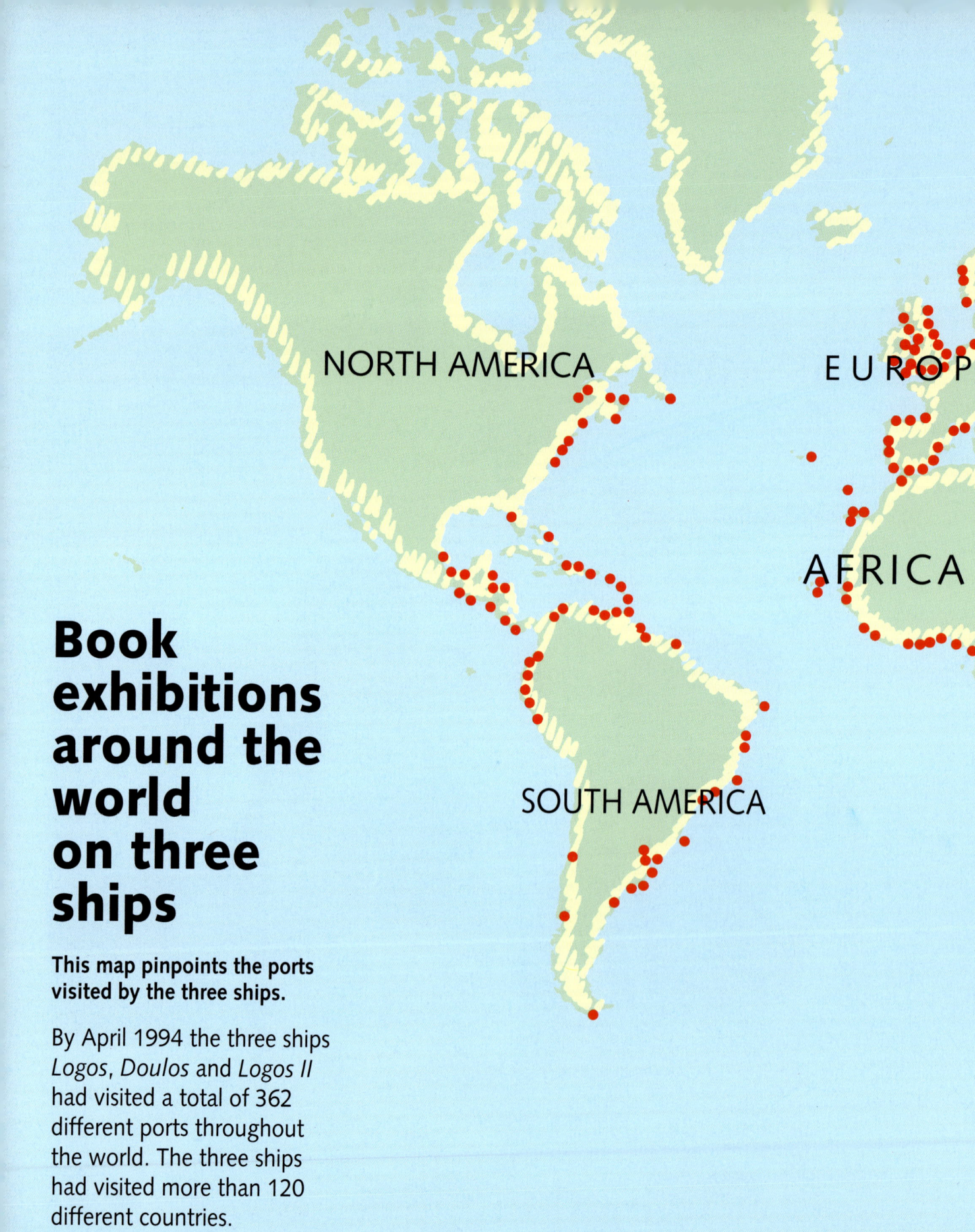

Book exhibitions around the world on three ships

This map pinpoints the ports visited by the three ships.

By April 1994 the three ships *Logos*, *Doulos* and *Logos II* had visited a total of 362 different ports throughout the world. The three ships had visited more than 120 different countries.

22

ASIA

MIDDLE EAST

AUSTRALASIA

23

Communicating via the ship's telephone.

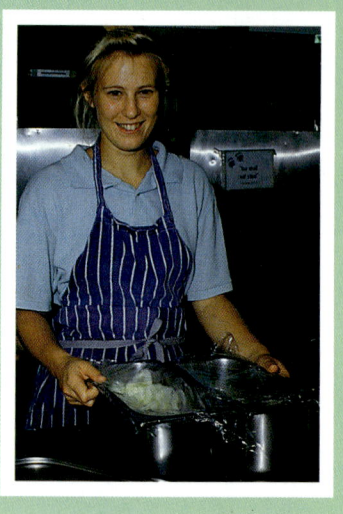

Above: On the bridge of *Logos II*.
Above right: In the galley.

Captain and Chief Mate.

Skilled personnel help maintain the ships.

Meet the crew

The ships have to comply with international regulations in every way. This includes sailing with the right number of qualified seamen on board. As on other passenger ships, most of these men and women work in one of three departments: deck, engine or catering.

In command, of course, is the captain. His is the ultimate legal responsibility for the safety and effective operation of the ship. Four stripes on the shoulder of his uniform indicate his position.

The chief mate is in charge of the deck department. His department is responsible for navigation, safety and external maintenance.

The engine department is headed by the chief engineer. The engine department is responsible for the ship's structure, machinery and electrical equipment.

Catering
The chief steward, in charge of the catering department, is responsible for the hotel arrangements on board. This includes food buying, preparation and serving, laundry, cabin assignments and cleaning of public areas.

Three other officers are directly accountable to the captain: the purser, the radio officer and the medical officer.

Left: Constant maintenance is necessary.
Far left: Overseeing loading into the hold.

Left: Checking the dials in the engine room.
Far left: In the engine room.

Using precision sextants, crew members plot the ship's position.

Line-up people

Weeks before one of the ships is due in port, a small team of line-up people goes ahead to prepare the way. Their job is to obtain all the necessary permissions for the ship's visit: permission to dock at a good berth, permission for crew and staff to disembark, permission for the selling of books, and permission for local residents to come aboard, etc. Line-up people also work with local pastors and civic leaders to plan the most effective programme for that port. Contacting local media to publicize the visit is another part of the line-up team's responsibility.

Logos II

The loss of *Logos* in 1988 came as a great shock. At the ships' headquarters in Germany, phone calls and letters poured in from around the world. In them a common theme was repeated again and again: *Logos* must be replaced. Its work cannot be lost.

Gifts poured in as well. Enough gifts to purchase in October of that same year a Spanish car ferry that had been operating between Spain and North Africa. Larger than *Logos*, but smaller than *Doulos*, she was 109.55 metres long, 4,804 tons gross register, and was able to accommodate 198 crew and staff. Furthermore, her layout could be altered to construct an auditorium seating 400 people, and a smaller one that could accommodate 100.

Carrying on
By general agreement the new ship carried on not only the work of the lost ship but its name as well. She was christened *Logos II*.

Like the other ships, she too was laid up for an extended period of renovation, which ended just at the time communism was beginning to crumble in Europe. In her first months of sailing she was welcomed into East Germany, Poland and the USSR, with her books and her message of hope, a living example of people from many countries, languages and cultures being able to live and work together in harmony and good will.

Life boat drill at sea.

EBE – Educational Book Exhibits.

Logos II at sea.

The captain of Logos II.

Meet the staff

While the qualified seamen on the ships count as 'crew', the other members of the ships' company are classed as 'staff'. The staff ensure that non-nautical aspects of the ship's life run smoothly.

What happens when a major disagreement arises between people on board? Or when a young person on the ship needs help in working through a personal problem?

Perhaps they will go to the ship director for counsel.

Ship director
While the captain concerns himself primarily with nautical aspects of the ship, the director looks out for the well-being and development of the people on board, and ensures the smooth and

Scandinavian staff.

Welcome aboard!

Staff in national dress.

A German staff member.

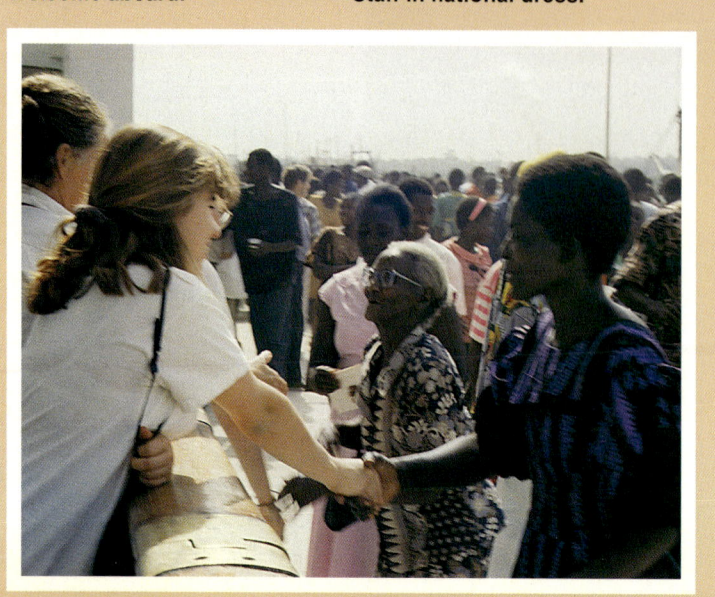

effective functioning of the ship's programme in a port.

No passengers!
The ship director, like many others on board who are involved in non-nautical work, is not considered crew but staff. Passenger ships generally carry paying passengers, but the 'passengers' on *Logos II* and *Doulos* work on their ships. For convenience, they are called staff instead of passengers.

Normal passenger ships have deck, engine and catering departments; these ships have a fourth, the ministry department. It deals with matters related to the function of the ship rather than the technical and practical work of running the ship.

Ministry department
Some of the staff who work in this department plan seminars, conferences and other meetings on board and ashore. Other staff work in the book exhibition on deck or organize the storage of books in the holds in the depths of the ship. Still others are involved in the training of the ships' workers.

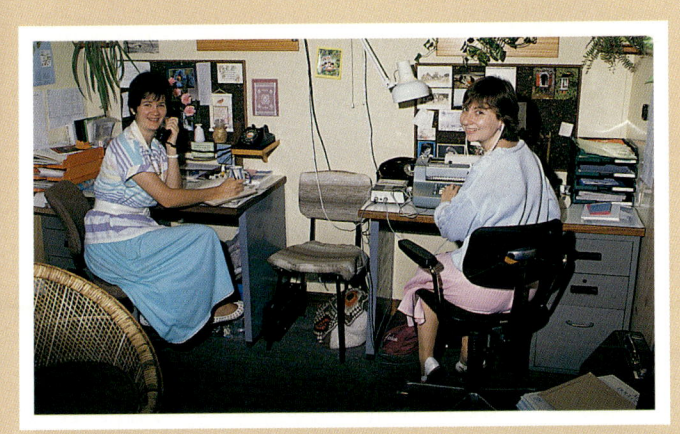

Office staff.

A visiting group in Africa.

A staff member from Taiwan.

The on-board nursery.

Staff from Papua New Guinea and South Africa.

29

Behind the scenes

As the work of the ships grew larger and busier, the leaders realized that they needed to set up a co-ordinating office. In 1980 this office was opened in Mosbach, near Stuttgart, Germany.

Each of the ships is a beehive of activity. Their nerve-centre, however, lies far away in a quiet little town in southern Germany. There in Mosbach about twenty men and women from several countries work at the headquarters to co-ordinate and manage the work of the two ships.

When an officer or other necessary crew person leaves the ship, the headquarters team must find a replacement. When someone wants to know more about the work, he can write to the Mosbach office for information. If he decides to join one of the ships, the Mosbach staff will process his application and provide him with orientation for the ship.

Is an alteration or replacement part needed for one of the ships? If the matter can't be handled on the ship itself, the marine superintendent in Mosbach will provide technical support.

Are food supplies on one of the ships running low? What cannot be obtained locally at a good price is ordered from elsewhere, usually from Europe, by the Mosbach staff and shipped out in huge containers along with other supplies.

Want to send a letter to someone on one of the ships? Don't send it directly to the ship. The chances are that it will miss connections and take months to catch up with the ship – if it ever does! Send it to the ships' headquarters and let the experienced postal person there take responsibility for forwarding it on to the right place at the right time.

These are just a few of the varied responsibilities shouldered by the support team at the ships' headquarters in Mosbach, Germany.

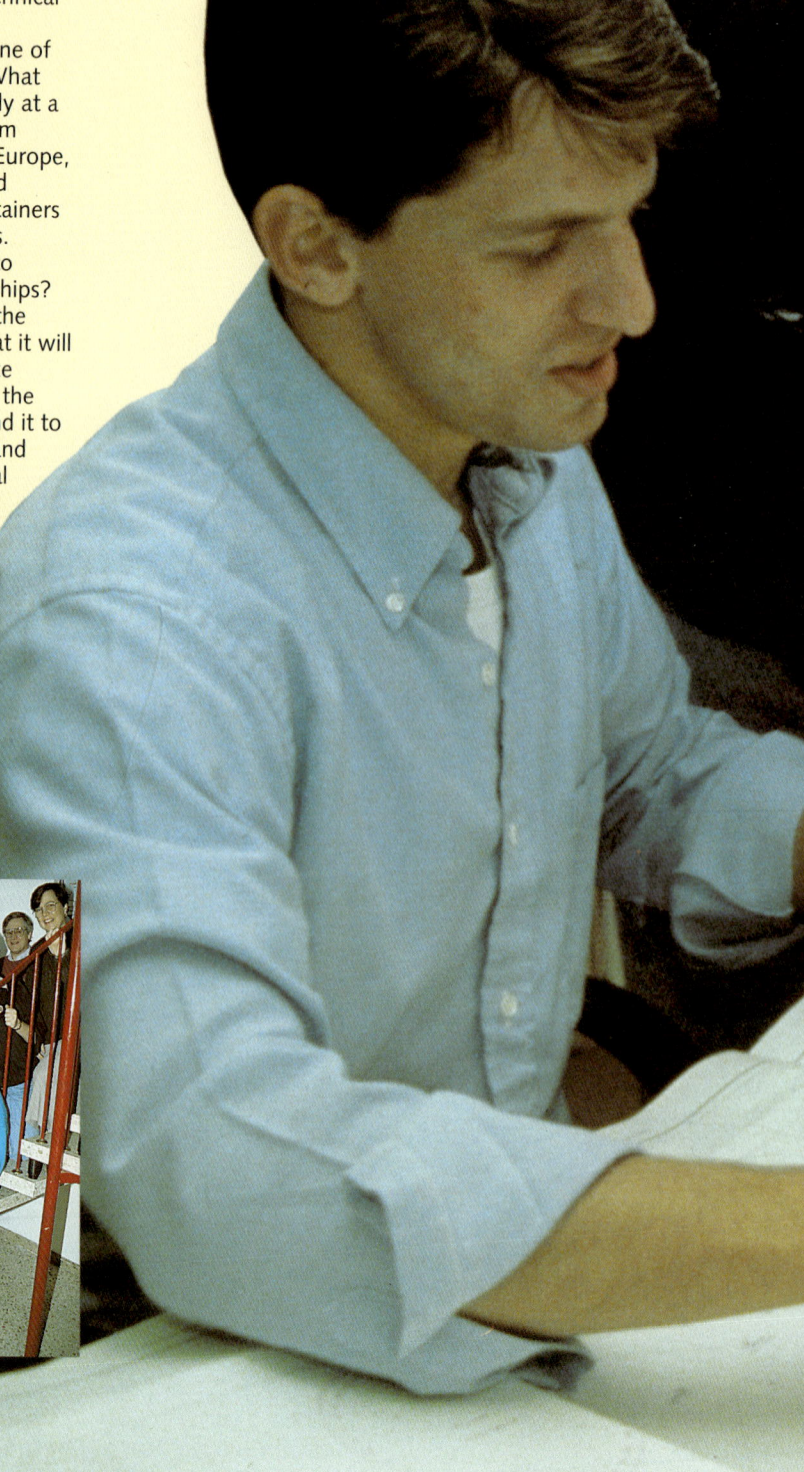

Below: Phone and fax are vital to ship-to-shore comunications.
Below right: The team at Mosbach.

The Mosbach office, near Stuttgart, Germany.

If you would like to know more . . .

As you will have discovered from this booklet, the story of these unusual ships is continually developing. As the enterprise grew from its tiny beginnings, new ideas were adopted for operating more effectively.

New regulations
New regulations now require a larger number of qualified seamen aboard each ship. The ships, as always, must be kept in good condition and equipment must be constantly updated. *Doulos* recently underwent a conversion of her electrical system from DC to AC, which should enable her to continue operating into the twenty-first century.

People matter
The ships themselves, however, are only tools to use in reaching out to people. People are what matter most. The ships' officers, crew and staff are committed to serving people and are continually looking for ways to improve that service.

How to keep in touch
If you are interested in receiving regular news about the ships, about the people on board and the places they are visiting, or about events taking place during visits in port, write requesting the regular newsletter, *Ship to Shore*.

Ship to Shore
OM Ships
Postfach 1565
D74819 Mosbach
Germany

Dale Rhoton, Ships' Director.